NO˙

MW00881517

The Characteristics Of The Male Gender Revealed

Olivier Heward

Table of Contents

Introduction

Chapter 1.......The Male Gender.

Chapter 2.......The Divinity Of The Male.

Chapter 3........The Purpose Of The Male Gift.

Chapter 4........Manhood.

Chapter 5........Second Dream.

Chapter 6........God's Concerns About The Male Gender.

Chapter 7.........The Voice Of A Male.

Chapter 8.........Sexual Sin.

Chapter 9.........Prayer To Break Soul Ties.

Chapter 10........Male Confidence.

Chapter 11.........Standard Change.

Chapter 12.........Exploring The Mind Of God.

Chapter 13.........Man's Territory.

Chapter 14.........Inquire In His Temple.

Chapter 15:........Poems.

Chapter 16:........Ultimate Change.

Chapter 17.........Declarations.

All rights reserved. No part of this book may be reproduced or transmitted in any form or by any means, electronic or mechanical- including photocopying, recording, or by an information storage and retrieval system, without permission in willing from the author of this book.

Scripture quotations are from the King James Version of the Holy Bible unless otherwise indicated.

Copyright 2024 by Olivier Heward.

Introduction

Deuteronomy 31:8 states that God will never leave us nor forsake us.

This book is based on my life story and struggles as a young boy growing up in the Caribbean island, the beautiful island of Saint Martin.

I want to first thank God for giving me the ability and inspiration to write this book. I also want to thank my wife, Cathy Gena Heward, my mother, Similienne Richardson Heward.

My sisters: Prophetess Patricia Joseph, Prophetess Congré Heward Olivia, Prophetess Oberlé Andréa, Pastor Jaky Cauvi.

My brothers: François Partricio, Merciris and Alain Heward and the entire family. My adopted nephew, Rémikio Rogers, a very genuine and God-fearing young man.

My special friends: Darissa Bique Leopold Merrick and Woodley Gisele.

I honor:

My spiritual dad, Apostle Eric Melwani and his wife, Pastor Janet Melwani who contribute to my life with many prayers and impartations. This book could not have become a reality without him, his wisdom, his love for others and his many teachings especially his teachings on The Holy Spirit. From his teaching and close relationship with the Holy Spirit and exploring the depths of The Holy Spirit, a book was birthed, entitled, 'Beloved Holy Spirit, My Best Friend'.

I honor Pastor Toulon Orlando.

I honor Apostle Ludwig Hodge and Prophetess Amanda Hodge.

I am so grateful to have these wonderful servants of God in my life.

Joshua 1:5,

"There shall not any man be able to stand before thee all the days of thy life: as I was with Moses, so I will be with thee: I will not fail thee, nor forsake thee."

This strong statement was given to me by The Holy Spirit to reassure and anchor me to have a victorious outcome.

As a young boy growing up, I always liked having friends and company, but I was suffering from severe rheumatism. Whenever I was playing with my cousins or alone, I used to get a pain in my heart for hours. I had to stay still in one place until it passed. Every twenty-one days I received an injection. The doctor told my mom that I will grow out of it once I continued the treatment. That was the beginning of my suffering. I used to sleep on one side of my body when I felt the pain in my heart. As the youngest in my family, like they say, I was the mama boy. Everywhere she went she took me. She was very concerned and protective. I was a boy that everyone liked but I was lacking something, inwardly.

This book was birthed and inspired from within the depth of the belly of the whale; being afflicted for more than ten years with chronic insomnia and depression. I embraced the Word of Hope steadfastly, but still asked myself, "why is this happening to me"?

Because God had given me the ability to endure. His word says that He will never leave me nor forsake me. That word is so impressive.

Hebrews 12:2,

"Looking unto Jesus the author and finisher of our faith; who for the joy that was set before him endured the cross, despising the shame, and is set down at the right hand of the throne of God."

We must endure all things no matter the situation. The outcome will be glorious if we remain in the faith.

Hebrews 11:6a,

"But without faith it is impossible to please him:"

HEBREWS 12:8,

"But if ye be without chastisement, wherefore all are partakers, then ye are bastards, and not sons."

It does not mean that it is God's will for you to be sick, poor, etc.

Our perspective must be from the point of view that we are perfected from glory to glory until we behold the beauty of the Lord and become his image and likeness.

We are partakers of his holiness according to The Word.

Hebrews 12:11,

"Now no chastening for the present seemeth to be joyous but grievous: nevertheless afterward it yieldeth the

peaceable fruit of righteousness unto them which are exercised thereby."

In this context, the word "exercise" means discipline.

The Male Gender

Why does the Bible refer to God in masculine terms?

This is the way God has chosen to reveal himself to us. God is never described with sexual characteristics in the Scriptures, but He does consistently describe Himself in the masculine gender. While God contains all the qualities of both male and female genders, He has chosen to present Himself with an emphasis on the masculine qualities of fatherhood: protection, direction, strength etc.....

One famous Christian scholar, C. S. Lewis, suggested that gender is far deeper than our human distinctions reveal. He suggested that God is so masculine that we all are feminine in relation to Him.

If this is true, it might explain why the church is referred to as the bride of Christ, though it is composed of men and women[i].

Psalm 82:6,

"I have said, Ye are gods; and all of you are children of the most High."

God calls us, male and female, "gods."

God has given us the ability to produce His own characteristics. I can say, His own flavour. We are gods to answer his calling.

God used Moses as a god.

Exodus 7:1, "And the LORD said unto Moses, See, I have made thee a god to Pharaoh: and Aaron thy brother shall be thy prophet."

It is clear that the male gender is an image of God's divinity.

In conclusion, the male gender is God's divinity. The male gender is sacred.

The Divinity Of The Male

In being divine, we must live a sacred and holy lifestyle.

Males are carrying the divinity which is the seed and that is why the enemy is raging war so hard against the male gender, to disrupt God's original plan for the male gender.

Homosexually is the primary tool the enemy uses to blaspheme the male gender of

God's creation. The enemy uses this strategy to get to God's divinity.

It is not just about a physical condition. It is also a spiritual condition. It goes way deeper than just an emotional feeling or the saying that a male gender is trapped in a woman's body, or I'm so confused about my gender, or I'm sexually attracted to the same sex, etc.

This is just the small picture where man fell. The big picture is that Satan is targeting the divinity of God by using our bodies, minds and wills and we must face the reality of this truth so that we can escape the big lies of the enemy. To escape his trap, we must replace his lies with the truth of God's word.

The Purpose Of The Male Gift

God ordained this gift to the male gender to know how to carry His glory as a principle of the kingdom, the prescribed way, the gift of dominion. God gave the male the grace to dominate from creation. God attributed to Adam that gift. Today, some people see it as authority. The difference is that authority is power and dominion is rulership.

God entrusted us, the males, to carry that gift so that we can be capable to manage, do the work and uphold the role of being the head.

To dominate is to be creative, to expand, to create how God created, to create solutions, to create conditions, to create changes, etc.

The purpose of the gift is to carry the ark of God, and you must carry it well.

We read the experience of Uzzah as recorded in **2 Samuel 6: 3-7,**

"And they set the ark of God upon a new cart, and brought it out of the house of Abinadab that was in Gibeah: and Uzzah and Ahio, the sons of Abinadab, drave the new cart.

4 And they brought it out of the house of Abinadab which was at Gibeah, accompanying the ark of God: and Ahio went before the ark.

5 And David and all the house of Israel played before the LORD on all manner of instruments made of fir wood, even on harps, and on psalteries, and on timbrels, and on cornets, and on cymbals.

6 And when they came to Nachon's threshingfloor, Uzzah put forth his hand to

the ark of God, and took hold of it; for the oxen shook it.

7 And the anger of the LORD was kindled against Uzzah; and God smote him there for his error; and there he died by the ark of God."

In Moses' time, they carried it on the priests' shoulders. Staves were made to carry the ark because no man was allowed to touch the ark.

Apart from the gift of the Holy Spirit which is the inheritance of a born again believer, both male and female, the male gender has a specific gift, the gift of upholding God's divinity, which is the gift of dominion. The gift of dominion is not to abuse or have dictatorship over others or to be macho or to be God's equal, but it's a gift to uphold God's governance on earth.

The male gender is responsible for his family, ministry, nations, etc. The male gender is accountable to God directly.

Manhood

Growing up as a young boy, I felt and was rejected. I also felt condemned. Then to add icing on the cake, I felt guilty because of the lifestyle I once lived as a bisexual person. Most of my adolescent life I felt different and that dragged me into a dark pit. The journey was traumatic. I felt that even God cut me off. But each time I was drawn back to that pit and sink back to my sins, I found inner strength to go to Jesus and cry out. I was being criticized and pass for shame. My story was the talk of the town. I lost sleep and confidence. One night I fell asleep and dreamt that Jesus came to me and blew wind in my face and I was revived. From that day I told myself that

God is not like man. He loved me in spite of my failures. It gave me strength and confidence in God in that He upheld me with His righteous right hand. I needed a righteous right hand but no one was able except Jesus Christ Himself .

Second dream

I was in this big room waiting. I had an appointment with the Lord. My sister was busy with her appointment with the Lord and I was telling myself that's a really long appointment that my sister was having, God must have forgotten me and forsaken me. When my sister's time was up, there came a little boy, waiting also, and when his time came to go inside with the Lord, he too stayed much longer than my sister. I said to myself, "that's it, God has forsaken me". I began to accuse myself of all of my sins and mistakes while I kept waiting and waiting.

Then suddenly I heard the Lord say, "Olivier my faithful", and I looked at Him with a surprised look. He then asked me, "why are you surprised" . I told him, "Lord I am not worthy". He said to me, "It is only you who said that you are not worthy. I didn't forsake you".

This was not to give me a red light to sin, my people. But God knows every man's heart. He saw my tears and heard my cries and most of all He knew my faithfulness. It was only then that I understood what He meant by me being faithful. I never separated myself from prayer or destitution for assistance and change. I never stopped even though I was called all sorts of names, labels and stigmatized.

Isaiah 50: 7-9,

"⁷For the Lord GOD will help me;
therefore shall I not be confounded:
therefore have I set my face like a flint,
and I know that I shall not be ashamed.

⁸He is near that justifieth me; who will
contend with me? let us stand together:
who is mine adversary? let him come
near to me.

⁹Behold, the Lord GOD will help me; who
is he that shall condemn me? lo, they all
shall wax old as a garment; the moth
shall eat them up."

Flint, a very hard, dark rock, is used
figuratively in the Bible to express
hardness, as in the firmness of horses'
hoofs.

You are who God says you are, faithful.

God's Concerns About The Male Gender

God was concerned about Adam's loneliness in the garden. God didn't create Eve for His own glory, but, she was created to be the man's helper, comforter, encourager, to have his back. God thus created a solution for Adam to be complete.

God was so concerned about Adam that God surprised him with His beautiful creation, which was the woman, Eve. The angels saw how God expressed his love for Adam that they wondered: what is it about the male gender that God was so mindful of them?

Psalm 8:4,

"What is man, that thou art mindful of him? and the son of man, that thou visitest him"?

The word visitest means: to attend.

God told Adam to name all the creatures, call them however you see them and I God will be pleased.

What a privilege it is for God to choose the male gender to put a name and a title to things according to His perfect will for man .

Psalm 8:6,

"Thou madest him to have dominion over the works of thy hands; thou hast put all things under his feet:"

The Voice of a Male

Male voices are usually deeper; males have thicker cords. The male vocal folds are between 17 mm and 25 mm in length. The female vocal folds are between 12.5 mm and 17.5 mm long. The difference in vocal fold size between men and women means that their voices have a different pitch.

A father's voice is a key note in a home that plays a very important role. It gives awareness to exercise stability and good senses because of the level of dominance that God gave him.

There is something inside your mouth that's very powerful; it's your tongue. It's given to you by God to form words; words with which to control, create or recreate the circumstances of your life.

James 3:6 says the tongue is a fire. The power for any change that you desire is in your tongue. Jesus said you shall have what you say, **Mark 11:23.**

If you speak confusing words, the result is that your life will be confusing because you are giving confusing signals. Words are spiritual elements. They do not die. That is why Jesus said, **"But I say unto you, That every idle word that men shall speak, they shall give account thereof in the Day of judgment." Matthew 12:36.**

One day, all your words will be shown to you by God, as to what they built, what they created, the image of your life and the circumstances of your life created by your words.

The most important thing in your life is your words. Your words will decide the quality of your life on earth. Your words will decide your relationship with God, your relationship with human beings, and where you go eternally: heaven or hell. No one else can determine the quality of your life. It is all going to come from your words.

For instance, when some people are excited, they will say: "If you continue this way, you'll kill me!" Or some others will say, "This troublesome child will kill me some day!" Or, "Look at poor me." Unfortunately, such people do not realize the power and importance of their words. Death and life are in the power of the tongue... **Proverbs 18:21.**

Sexual Sin

Edwin L. Cole said in his book, **Maximized Manhood:**

"In this modern era, we don't have sins. We have problems. We have psychologized the gospel, and in the process we have eliminated the word sin from our vocabulary" .

"Human sorrow is when we are only sorry for getting caught .Godly sorrow is when we are sorry for the sin, and have a desire to be rid of it".

"The desire to give in to sin is a choice to fail". [ii]

We must not despise the spirit of grace.

Hebrews 10:29,

"Of how much sorer punishment, suppose ye, shall he be thought worthy, who hath trodden under foot the Son of God, and hath counted the blood of the covenant, wherewith he was sanctified, an unholy thing, and hath done despite unto the Spirit of grace?"

Chasing my own lustful desires became a fantasy and a selfish gain. Those desires had absolutely nothing to do with God's desire for my life.

I was fulfilling Satan's agenda and not God's agenda. It became a battle within. Often, I couldn't sleep a certain hour of the night If I did indulge in sin at night time. It had to be early in the day so that the previous night's activity would have had enough time to wear off in order for me to sleep better at night,

otherwise I would be tormented all night. Even though I knew that God would forgive me, I still used to carry that guilt. It was my disobedience that used to affect me. I described it as guilt because of the shame before.

I realized that spending time with God and praying in tongues to restore my foundation in Christ used to occupy my mind because I had lost my covering. I read once that there was this particular man who used to pray an hour in tongues every day. I kept telling my wife that I had a gap from the time my health condition fell apart. I was experiencing this gap not having a sense of life and purpose. I struggled with this condition for years. One day the Holy Spirit dropped in my spirit: "if you are lost in your ways and senses being in the gap that you are in now, instead of trying to find back your way and senses, use this gap to build a new way, to start a new beginning with God and realize that old things have passed away" .

I still wanted to feel like me again, so, when I received that word I began changing my mind about desiring the same taste for that old, sinful life. I had to live with the now even though it was not comfortable.

Sin does not ease pain, it worsens it. Only Jesus Christ can ease the pain when you yield to righteous living and allow God to change you. .

Prayer To Break Soul Ties

Every padlock that is bound together with sexual partners, I command it to break in Jesus' name.

Every burden from emotional lash be annulled now in Jesus' name.

I cast off all spells, bewitchments and charms in Jesus' name.

Every word of seductive seed planted in my life, I remove it by its roots in Jesus' name.

I command all pain to dissolve in Jesus' name.

I break all soul ties with darkness in Jesus' name.

I am redeemed from darkness to God's marvelous light in Jesus' name.

Every curse that came upon me by sowing wild oats, I confess and command it to break in Jesus' name.

Amen. Thank you Lord for answering prayers.

Male Confidence

Men are the product of God's imagination.

God was so confident in making man that He formed him from the dust and was pleased to breathe His breath into him so that man became a living image of God.

Man was crowned with glory. God placed within him confidence even though he came from the dust. God took a simple element to express value and meaning.

We are qualified because God qualified us. It is not by our own selves. The dust cannot do anything without the breath of God.

Man must always remember where he came from. Our original state is dust. It is also a form of humility for us to walk humbly before God because we are only dust. Man can only be confident because God made him confident.

There is no sense of pride in the dust.

Pride has no life in the dust.

This is why some people get confused about being prideful and having confidence.

Our confidence stems from the fact that God chose to form us, from dust, and, if God is for us who can be against us. Therefore, our confidence is of God's standards.

Hebrews 10:35-36, "**Cast not away therefore your confidence, which hath great recompence of reward. For ye have need of patience, that, after ye have done the will of God, ye might receive the promise.**"

God called us out from the dust to fulfil His purpose.

Only God can do what He does.

Our lives must be based on who God is, not only because he turned dust to man, but because He sits on the throne for ever and ever.

We are confident because God has given us the ability to be.

Although we were formed from the dust, we are not limited to the dust.

God did an extreme work, He is the mighty God, the only true and wise God.

We cannot trace or transcend His greatness.

The dust is nothing without God's breath.

The Word of God declares :

Isaiah 38:18, "For the grave cannot praise thee, death can not celebrate thee: they that go down into the pit cannot hope for thy truth."

Psalm 30:9, "What profit is there in my blood, when I go down to the pit? Shall the dust praise thee? shall it declare thy truth?"

Let your confidence rise from the dust.

Accept that you come from the dust and your confidence shall rise from there.

When most people hear about dust they usually have a negative image about it especially when people get a prophetic word. They usually point out the dust as a weight, something dirty, something that is dormant; which is not wrong, but there is also a positive side about dust. But, starting today and moving forward, you will place value on dust just like God placed value on the dust, because, it is His breath.

Standard Change

Psalm 34: 4-6,

"I sought the LORD, and he heard me, and delivered me from all my fears. 5They looked unto him, and were lightened: and their faces were not ashamed. 6This poor man cried, and the LORD heard him, and saved him out of all his troubles."

In this passage the words "poor man" signify humility and meekness.

As he sought God with a right heart, God came through for him and saved him from all his troubles.

Standard change happens when you decide to turn everything over to God.

You now allow Him to work on your life because you finally came to the end of yourself.

You keep trying and trying and frustration builds up. With all the deliverance prayers and counselling you did over the years, the habits and addictions seem to increase while the perversion and the fantasy still haunts you.

What more needs to be done? You fast, you promise God, you sow seed for change, you wrote down pages of declarations but it seems like God is silent .

As you set standard change, you cannot allow pressures to challenge you, to break you and set you back, or allow relationships or family or even habitual sin or anything to break your standard change. Let nothing separate you from the goal that you have set to please God while going through the steps.

When the dog keeps going back to his own vomit, it is not healthy.

You can call on God to help you to get out of habits and situations. As long as you decide not to give up your idol or your sin, God will not be able to help you. It must be conditional. For years we have watered down the word of God. Many have gone through deliverance to cast out devils but it wasn't a matter of devils but a matter of bad habits. Some people I know smoked for years and just decided to stop and they did a tremendous work on themselves. No one laid hands on them or cast out any devils. You cannot put all the blame on devils; you are just making things harder for yourself and for God's servants. You just need to read the word and work on your habits. The word of God is life and spirit.

Isaiah 59: 1-2, "Behold, the LORD's hand Is not shortened, that it cannot save; neither his ear heavy, that it cannot hear: 2 But your iniquities have separated between you and your God, and your sins have hid his face from you, that he will not hear."

We all have to be accountable and responsible on that day when the Lord will ask you and me what did we do to make our situation become a miracle.

The Bible says that God makes ways of escape. Did you take the way of abstinence? Did you take the way of submitting? Which way did you take?

When we depart from God He allows evil spirits to come upon us.

1 Samuel 16:14, "But the Spirit of the LORD departed from Saul, and an evil spirit from the LORD troubled him."

Prayer: Psalm 119: 107,114, 116-117.

107 "I am afflicted very much: quicken me, O LORD, according unto thy word."

114 "Thou art my hiding place and my shield: I hope in thy word."

116"Uphold me according unto thy word, that I may live: and let me not be ashamed of my hope."

117 "Hold thou me up, and I shall be safe: and I will have respect unto thy statues continually."

Exploring The Mind Of God

We can imagine the thoughts of God and His great imagination and unlimited vision. In Him we have all the hope and peace we will ever need. When we are hopeless and void of anticipation, God has already completed and filled that void. His word concerning us says that He gives us an expected end and also comes along with His peace.

Jeremiah 29:11,

"For I know the thoughts that I think toward you saith the LORD, thoughts of

peace, and not of evil, to give you an expected end."

God is qualified for this job. He is the Potter and we are the clay.

The Potter's house is always at work. New vessels are made and old, damaged, vessels are restored afresh.

In times past, vessels used to be carried on the head or on the back with a strap tied to the shoulders. It demonstrates how Christ, who is the head of the church, carries us His vessels on His head and when we are hopeless, burdened and broken, He carries us on His back. He ties us to His shoulders to brace us and He carries all the load.

God truly cares and loves us, His sons and daughters.

He fits the perfect description of a father.

Man's Territory.

Men were given the ground to work when man fell.

Adam became creative when God told him that he had to work the ground and from it, he was going to receive his substance. It perhaps felt and looked really hard, especially from the position he was in before the fall. He did not have to toil neither reap. Just like the birds of the air, the Heavenly Father fed him.

Adam became creative to plow the ground. He sure did catch up on the sowing and reaping.

In life, when you find yourself in a situation and you hit rock bottom as a result of your choice, you then have to become creative to work something out.

You will become a student and your situation becomes your teacher; you've been launched out to the deep.

You are in the belly of the fish. What will be your response?

Enlarge your territory. Work the ground to produce wealth; to generate income so that you can reap the harvest.

Inquire In His Temple

To inquire in the Lord's temple means to seek the face of the Lord, to consult Him in matters of difficulty; to search and seek after the knowledge of divine things and to ask for God's blessings of grace, for which you are inquiring after for God to bestow on you.

Poems

The Flesh:

Beyond the flesh, reflects the mind

Vanity of my flesh, a silent scream that's painful beneath facts.

My flesh is infected with thorns of my past.

The memory of Sodom wanting to bring
back Gomorrah.

The thorns keep pressing my heart.

Habits that invade my soul, unawares.
Actions that cost me my life and my friends.

Vanity of my soul

The guilt of my flesh

The harmful flesh

The corrupt, sophisticated flesh

The perishing flesh

The yielding and searching for satisfaction
resides in my flesh

Overwhelmed with collections that is
snapped between consciousness.

I need time to digest and conduct the accurate flesh; to remind myself that the flesh has been crucified.

True re-created habits lead me to declare victory.

Olivier Heward

Poem

Treasure:

My treasure is my heart

I will not invest it in pleasure

But I will invest it in my future

As I live my life as an adventure,

I mature

I live the scriptures

I cease from being captured

Knowing that whatsoever I do, my life will be measured as a living sculpture.

A description of God's picture

Life pressure, quality that is precious to me

To rapture my soul to the next level beyond the impossible.

The Ultimate Change

The billionaire Grant Cardone once said: "change is not easy , staying the same is terrible"[iii].

Satan comes to kill, steal and destroy. He has been stealing from men long enough. He stole our visions, blinded our minds, dull our stars, stole our time with things that bind us such as: drugs, alcohol, sexual immorality, gambling, social media, video games, wrong friendships, procrastination, ignorance and even the monies we work hard for.

Joel 1:4, "That which the palmerworm hath left hath the locust eaten; and that which the locust hath left hath the cankerworm eaten; and that which the cankerworm hath left hath the caterpillar eaten."

Caterpillars are known for being larval insects with big appetites. The Antheraea Polyphemus in particular is able to eat eighty-six times its own body mass in fifty-six days

Sometimes we work multiple jobs to make ends meet but suddenly some bad habit emerges which can come in a form of lust and strip you of your finances and steals your monies. When I was out there having worldly fun with my friends, we would go to the movies to hang out then eat then go from club to club then hit the casino, if we had any money left. By that time we became hungry again. Every one used to be broke; only a few stingy ones used to save a dollar or two. We called them stingy but they had some kind of radar to save something for rainy days. The caterpillar was on the hunt for those few who escaped. They were only to the level of the locust. The caterpillar is the last to pass and eat what's left. The caterpillar's purpose is to make sure that nothing is left. You end up living from paycheck to paycheck.

So, my advice to you is to invest those few dollars before the caterpillar gets it. That's the kind of destruction we risk when we do not yield to discipline and good conduct.

In this whole life time, we have been trying to figure out who are we actually, who am I, where am I going, how did I reach to this level and how can I get it right ?

To answer your question, it is simply an evil force that is controlling everything about you.

Declarations

The Spirit of God has made me and the breath of the Almighty has given me life.

He put my feet in the stocks, He guides all my paths.

I have sinned and perverted that which was right, but, it did not benefit me. God will deliver my soul from going into the pit, and my life shall see the light.

I will sing praise to thee, and not be silent. O LORD my God, I will give thanks unto thee forever.

I break the jaws of my enemies and pull out the spoil from their teeth.

For it is Your fire O God that consumes to destruction and uproot all my enemies.

I abstain from the passions of my flesh which wage war against my soul.

For Your commandment O God, this day, is not hidden from me neither is it far from me. Your word is very near to me. It is in my mouth and my heart and I am able to do it.

I am delivered from the lust of the flesh, the lust of the eyes and the pride of life.

Your word is a lamp to my feet and a light to my path.

You, O God, have heard my prayers and have seen my tears. Behold, you will heal me.

Deuteronomy 30:11, 2 Kings 20:5, Job 29: 17, Job 31:12,

Job 33:4, 11,27-28; Psalm 30:12, Psalm 119:105, 1 Peter

i Billy Graham Evangelistic Association: https://billygraham.org>answer

ii Edwin L. Cole, chapter 3, Maximized Manhood

iii Grant Cardone on LinkedIn #change #opportunities #growth

Made in the USA
Columbia, SC
24 October 2024

44594739R00030